Stories of Lo

E. L. Hoskyn

Alpha Editions

This edition published in 2024

ISBN : 9789362925015

Design and Setting By
Alpha Editions
www.alphaedis.com
Email - info@alphaedis.com

Contents

PREFACE

There are many kinds of ignorance which, for lack of time and opportunity, we may rightly tolerate in ourselves. Ignorance of the stories that cling around and beautify the home-place is not one of these. A place, indeed, is not a home unless human life has woven a thread of story through and through it. Happy are those who dwell as children in a place well clad with racy memories and legendary lore. The city-home of the London child is just such a place. Here we have a city with an old old history losing itself in the mists of time, and preserving itself in the memorials of its ancient sites and the tales that grow like ivy round its odd place-names. Of all this the careless city-dweller takes no note, but the London child should be a different kind of being. London stories are racy of London; they reflect its life in every age; and the London child is heir to them all.

The stories of London in this little book are interesting to everybody, whether young or old; they cannot fail to be so, because London is interesting, more or less, to everybody in the world. But the book is written more particularly for the children of London, so that they may not be careless city-dwellers, as so many are, but may grow up into real citizens of this great London, loving their old city in all its nooks and corners for its own dear sake, feeling it in all the twists and turns of its varied history, as if their life and its life were bound up in one.

But this is not all that the study of London's stories may do for the London child. The natural beginning of interest in history—including the literature that collects around it—arises out of interest in the story of the place in which we live. We walk about the place and picture the events of which we read as happening within it. The place is transfigured, is filled with life; and the story is transfigured too as seen against the background to which it really belongs. In the case of London, moreover, there is a good deal of useful work for the imagination to do in sufficiently restoring that background to its primitive simplicity. So the London child who knows the London stories thoroughly—so thoroughly as to be able to see them in their real setting, as they happened in that city by the river on the marshes in the olden time—has learnt to know how every other story, including the history proper of any other town or country, should be known.

Thus, the study of the home story is for each of us the true beginning of our education in that exercise of historical imagination on which our appreciation of history largely depends.

It is hoped that these Stories of London will be specially interesting to the London child, but not to him alone. The story of London is central in the story of England, and appeals to the interest of every English-speaking child.

SOPHIE BRYANT.

I.
SOME VERY OLD STORIES

The first story of London should tell who built it, and when, and why. But London is old, very old; it began before its builders had even thought of making books, and so its earliest history is written in the ground on which it stands, in its hills and valleys, its rivers and river-beds; and this is a kind of history which, if only we know how to read it, always tells the truth. Perhaps you are saying to yourself, "There is only one river in London, and that is the Thames; and there are no hills,—London is flat; and as for the ground, who has seen the real ground on which London stands? Is it not all built over, or paved with wood or stones or cement? How, then, can we learn anything from it?" Sometimes old worn-out buildings have to be pulled down to their very foundations so that new houses may be put in their places, or a tube-railway or a tunnel has to be made, or gas-pipes or electric wires have to be laid under the roads;—have you not seen navvies digging deep into the earth to do all these things? Then the secret things hidden in the ground are brought to light, and they teach us something of the very old history of the land.

Perhaps you know that the Hampstead and Highgate Hills lie four or five miles north of the Thames; and at about the same distance south of it are other hills, on one of which the Crystal Palace stands. Though we call the land between these hills the Thames Valley, it is not flat; and long ago, before London was built in it, it was much more uneven than it is now; for the more level roads are the easier it is for heavy carriages and carts to be pulled along them, so hollows have been filled up and hillocks cut down to make the ground as flat as possible. Even now, as you ride on the top of an omnibus through the long straight road called Oxford Street, if you watch carefully you may notice the rise and fall of the land,—a little hill, then a little valley, and so on. Once through each of these valleys a stream ran down to the Thames. Where are they now? Some of them are underground—arched over, built over, buried in the dark, out of sight. Look at the map on p. 11; there you will find one of these rivers, which ran from the Highgate Woods southward to the Thames. It was called the Fleet, and has given its name to Fleet Street.

NO. 3. IN WESTMINSTER ABBEY: THE TOMB OF EDWARD THE CONFESSOR WITH ITS VELVET COVERING See pages 17 and 22

There were also some low hills quite close to the north bank of the river. Let us fancy that we have gone back through the ages, many hundreds of years before ever the Romans came to this country, and that we are standing—you and I—facing the river on one of those hills, that on which St. Paul's now stands. What do we see? To our right, under its steep clay bank, so high it is almost a cliff, the Fleet runs on its way to the Thames; to our left is the hill; behind us, all the way up to the hills of Hampstead, are tangled forests, and in the low ground are wide marshes; and in front is the river. It is low-water; on either side of the stream are great stretches of mud and sand, wet marshy places, such as you may have seen at some place by the sea where the shore is very flat and the tide goes out very far. Beyond the marsh, on the southern shore, I think there is a wide shallow lake, for to this day some of the land there is below the level of the river at high-water. As we watch, look! a little rippling wave runs over the flats between the sand-banks; the tide has turned,—how fast it rises, how far it spreads! Before long the wide waste before us is covered with grey waters; it has become a great lake or sea. Nowadays embankments, such as you see in picture 1, keep the river in its place; but in the long-ago times of which we are thinking every high tide must have spread far and wide over what is now dry land.

NO. 4. THE FIRST CORONATION IN THE ABBEY See page 21

Could any people have wished to live in such a watery place? Yes, indeed they did; and under the bed of the Fleet River, near its mouth, traces have been found of their homes. That ancient people must have had many enemies,—other men who fought them, fierce wild animals, wolves and other creatures which have not lived in England for hundreds and hundreds of years; and to defend themselves that people had such poor weapons, perhaps made only of bronze; so they sought for a very safe dwelling-place. Down into the muddy bed of the river they drove great wooden posts, such posts as men drive down now into river or sea when they are building a pier. The worn tops of those old timbers have been found showing up through the soil where once the Fleet ran; and on them once rested a platform of wood on which houses were built. Is not this a piece of history written in the soil? The first men who tried to read it understood more easily the meaning of those worn old posts because to this day the brown people, who live in one of the great islands to the south-east of Asia, build their houses on just such platforms out over the water.

How long did the men of that far-off time live in these strange river-dwellings? That we do not know; it may have been for very many years. At last (so some learned men believe) they built for themselves a fort or stronghold on the high land near-by, perhaps where St. Paul's now stands, but more likely lower down the river, on the next hill; this stronghold may have been the beginning of London. If, as some people think, London means "The Fort of the Waters," or "The Lake Fort," was it not well named?

Up the river to this fort ships may sometimes have come, bringing merchants to buy pearls and skins of wild animals and slaves; and to pay for them with such things as the fierce Londoners of those days would like—a sharp axe or a gay necklace.

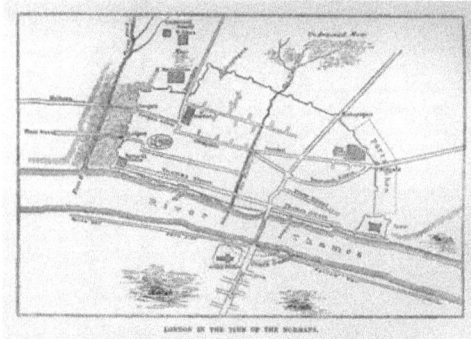

LONDON IN THE TIME OF THE NORMANS.

The written history of London does not begin until the Romans had conquered and were ruling the land, more than a hundred years after their great general, Julius Cæsar, had first come here. They found London only a little group of huts, very likely made of wickerwork plastered over with mud, and surrounded by a poor wall and ditch. How much they did for it! They built round it the great walls which you see marked in our little map; so strong were they that parts of their foundations and of the walls themselves have been found even of late years. And many other traces of the Romans have been found in London—coins, and weapons, and carvings. Near the Strand is a bath which once, perhaps, belonged to some Roman gentleman's fine house. There were many such houses in and about London; and many a time the beautiful pavements of these houses, and even the pavements of the old Roman streets, have been found in the City down below the present streets and houses. The Romans made great roads which stretched out north, south, east, and west, from London; and they built a bridge over the Thames. In those days the people across the English Channel, the Gauls and Italians, were far wiser than the wild people of Britain; and roads and bridges made it possible for their trade, skill and wisdom to come to the people of London. A flourishing city it became under the Roman rule.

The years passed on and evil days befell the Roman Empire; the wild fierce northern races attacked it, and the Roman soldiers had to leave Britain and go back to defend Italy. Then there came to this country also sad days of war and trouble, for the English came over the North Sea, fought and conquered the Britons, and at last settled here. Then came the Danes, and there was more war, more fighting. During these dreadful times we hear little of London.

At last Alfred became King. Do you remember how many good things he did for England? One of the best of them was that in the year 886, as the ancient Chronicle or history of our country tells us, he built London Town,—that is, he built again her walls and towers, and made her once more a strong city. Thus, with Alfred as her founder and protector, her later history begins. Year by year she grew greater and more important, until she became the greatest of all English cities and the capital of the land.

There is another and a very different story of Old London, and this is how it begins:—"Brute, about the yeare of the world 2855 and 1108 before the nativitie of Christ" (that is, before Christ was born,) "builded this city neare unto the riuer (river) now called Thames, and named it Troynouant"—that is, 'New Troy.' Now, this Brute belonged to the very same family as Romulus who built Rome; and he and his followers came across the sea to this island, in which then only a few giants were living, and he conquered them and took the land, and named it Britain after his own name, and his companions he called Britons.

There were more giants in Cornwall than in any other part of the land. One of them was called Goëmagot; he was so strong that he could pull up an oak-tree as if it were only a hazel-wand. Now there was a great fight between the Britons and the Cornish giants, and all the giants were killed but Goëmagot. Then he and a famous Briton fought together, and all men stood by to watch. At first it seemed that the giant would win for he wounded the Briton sorely; but, wounded as he was, the Briton heaved Goëmagot up on his shoulders, ran with him to the shore, and flung him headlong into the sea; and (so says the story) the rock from which he fell is called "The Giant's Leap" unto this day. All this happened near the place where Plymouth now stands. What has it to do with London? In the Guildhall, which is the Council Hall of London, are many statues of great and famous men, and here are also two great wooden giants called Gog and Magog; they are the City's giants. Once they used to be carried in the Lord Mayor's Show and in processions to make the people wonder. The older giant is said to be Goëmagot; the other, the Briton who hurled him headlong into the sea.

Long after Brute died, Belinus became King. Of all his wonderful history I can tell you only this,—he placed a great building in Trinovantum (that is, London,) upon the banks of the Thames, and the citizens called it, after his name, Billingsgate. Over it he built a huge tower, and under it a fair haven or quay for ships. "At last, when he had finished his days, his body was burned, and the ashes put up in a golden urn, which they placed with wonderful art on the top of the tower" which he himself had built. Have you ever heard of Billingsgate? It is the chief fish-market of London, and its wharf is the oldest on the Thames, so old that no one knows when fish were first landed and sold there.

Many years after Belinus built his great tower, Lud became King. He "not only repaired this Cittie" (that is, Trinovantum,) "but also increased the same with faire buildings, Towers and walles; and after his own name called it Caire Lud, as Lud's towne." And about sixty-six years before Christ was born he built a strong gate in the west part of the city, and he named it, in his own honour, Ludgate; and when he died his body was buried by this gate. Turn back to the little <u>map</u> of London on p. 11; there you will find Ludgate marked. St. Paul's Cathedral stands just to the east of it, on Ludgate Hill.

These stories were first written down by a Welsh priest called Geoffrey of Monmouth, who lived in the days of King Stephen; and long ago everyone believed they were true. Then came a time when people said what, perhaps, you are thinking, "These stories are only fairy-tales. Who made them up?" Well, Geoffrey of Monmouth said, in his book written nearly 800 years ago, that he had read them in a still older book which came out of Brittany. Who else had read this old book? No one, so Geoffrey said; so people left off believing them; they were put aside and forgotten. Now wise men think that they are really the old stories of our nation which have been passed down from father to son, and that perhaps the heroes of which they tell are the gods the people once worshipped, that Lud was a God of the Waters. If so, was it not very natural that he was worshipped in Old London on the shores of the Thames and the Fleet Rivers?

There is another hero, Bran the Blessed, of whom I must tell you. He too was King of the Isle of the Mighty, as Britain was called. He was so big no ship could contain him for he was like a mountain, and his eyes were like two lakes. In the end of his days he fought with the Irish in their own land until only he and seven of his followers were left alive, and he was wounded unto death. And he said to his followers, "Very soon I shall die; then cut off my head, and take it with you to London, and there bury it in the White Mountain looking towards France, and no foreigners shall invade the land while it is there." Much more he told them of the manner of their coming to London, and all that he said came true, so that many years passed away before in the White Mount, where the Tower now stands, they buried the head. There it lay until Arthur dug it up, for he said, "The strong arm should defend the land." He meant that the men of a nation should be its defence.

Arthur himself was proclaimed King in London. Perhaps you remember the old story of the child who was brought up so secretly that, when the King, his father, died, no one knew who was now the rightful King or, indeed, if there was one. Then, as Merlin the Magician had advised, the Archbishop of Canterbury called on all the great lords of the kingdom to come together in London; and there, one day, outside the greatest church in the City (was it St. Paul's, I wonder?) they saw a great stone with a sword sticking in it; and round about the stone, written in letters of gold, were these words:—"Whoso pulleth out this sword of this stone is right wise born King of England." The great lords tried to pull it out, and not one of them could do so; but young Arthur, who had come to town with his foster-father and foster-brother, pulled it out easily, not because he wanted to show that he was the King,—he does not seem to have known about this,—but because his foster-brother had sent him to fetch a sword and he could get no other. Thus, all men knew that he was "right wise born King of England."

NO. 5. A ROOM IN THE TOWER WHERE STATE PRISONERS
WERE LODGED.

NO. 6. SIR THOMAS MORE AND HIS DAUGHTER WATCH
THE CARTHUSIAN PRIORS GOING AWAY TO DIE. See page
26

II.
THE STORY OF WESTMINSTER ABBEY

Turn to the picture facing <u>p. 8</u>. If you have ever been in London, I think you will know that this is a picture of part of Westminster Abbey. Even if you have never seen the Abbey, perhaps you know that it is a very old and beautiful church near the River Thames in London. Imagine that you are standing near it now, and that you can see its old grey walls, and the grass and railings which separate it from the busy street with its motors and omnibuses, its carriages and carts. Now, with the roar of the streets in our ears, with the tall London buildings all around us, and busy people constantly hurrying past us, let us try to fancy what this spot was like in the very early times when we first hear of it.

Then the Thames was clear and fresh and full of fish, and many a red deer and other wild animal wandered along its banks and drank of its waters. About a mile and a half above London, where the river was wide and shallow, one of those little brooks of which I have told you ran into it; and here, where the waters of the brook and of the river met, was a bank of sandy gravel, which at high tide was an island, so it was called Thorney or Thorn Ey—the Island of Thorns—for it was all overgrown with thorn-bushes. Very lonely, very quiet, Thorney must have been.

Who first lived there, what kind of a dwelling-place they had, we do not really know. In later days the monks, whose home it then was, said that once the temple of a Roman god had stood there, and that when the Britons became Christians a good King built in its place a Christian church called the Abbey of St. Peter. Do you remember that, after the Romans left Britain, the English, who were still heathen, came over the North Sea and conquered the Britons and settled on their lands? The monks said that in those days of war and trouble the little Abbey of St. Peter was destroyed. Early in the seventh century, when the English also had learnt the Christian Faith, Sebert, King of the East Saxons, rebuilt the little abbey, and when he died he was buried there. So said the monks, and to this very day there is a grave in Westminster Abbey which is said to be Sebert's.

There is a strange story told about this ancient church. It was just finished, and the first Bishop of London, Mellitus, was to come on a certain Monday to consecrate it—that is, to set it apart for the service of God. The evening before a man called Edric was fishing in the river. Suddenly, on the southern bank, he saw a bright light; he pulled his little boat towards it, and saw standing by the water a strange-looking stately man, who pointed towards Thorney and said, "Ferry me, I pray thee, across to yonder place"; and Edric did so. As the stranger landed and went to the new church the air was filled with heavenly light, the church was "without darkness or shadow," and through the light angels came flying from the skies, and with their help the stranger held the solemn service of consecration. All this Edric heard and saw. Do you wonder that he forgot all about his fishing?

When the service was ended and, I suppose, the heavenly light had faded away and darkness again covered the place, the stranger came to Edric and asked for food. "Alas!" he answered, "I have none. I have not caught a single fish."

Then said the stranger, "I am Peter, Keeper of the Keys of Heaven. When the Bishop comes to-morrow, tell him that I, St. Peter, have consecrated my own church of St. Peter. Go thou out into the river; thou wilt catch many a fish, whereof the most part will be salmon. This I grant thee if thou wilt promise two things;—first, that never again wilt thou fish on Sunday; and, secondly, that thou wilt give one-tenth of thy fish to the Abbey of St. Peter."

Next day King Sebert and the Bishop of London came to Thorney. There, by the new church, with a salmon in his hand, Edric, the fisherman, was waiting to tell his story. Did they believe it? How could they help believing? for he showed them the marks of twelve crosses on the church, and the traces of the sacred oil and of the candles which the angels had held! There was nothing left for the Bishop to do but to declare that the church had been well and truly consecrated.

These are the wonderful stories the monks used to tell of their abbey. I suppose they loved it so much that they wanted people to think it as old and as wonderful as it could possibly be.

But now we have come to real history which we know to be true. In 1042 Edward, called the Confessor, became King of England. Englishmen long remembered him and what he looked like; his hair and beard were milky white, and his cheeks were red; he loved hunting and long services in church; and his people believed that the touch of his hand would heal the sick, and that God spoke to him in dreams and visions.

His father had been driven out of England by the Danes, and Edward had grown up in Normandy; so it came about that he loved the Normans, who were more courteous than the rude rough English. Yet I think he loved England too, for we are told that he made a vow to St. Peter that if ever he returned there in safety he would make a pilgrimage to the saint's grave in Rome.

He did not keep this vow; his people would not let him, for they said, "The journey to Rome is long and dangerous, and our King is very precious to us. We cannot let him go." But a man, even if he is a King, may not break a solemn vow, so Edward asked the Pope what he must do, and the Pope answered, "Stay at home and rule thy people; yet, as thou hast vowed to make a pilgrimage to Rome, do some other costly thing instead. Build a new church, or rebuild an old one in honour of St. Peter." And King Edward determined to rebuild the little church at Thorney, or Westminster as we must now call it; for the thorns had long since been cleared away, the sandy bank was no longer an island even at high-water, and pleasant meadows lay on either side of the river.

For fifteen years the work went on; Edward was so interested in it, so loved it, that he watched over and cared for every part of it. Now at last, at Christmas-time of the year 1065, the east end was finished. How eagerly the King looked forward to its consecration! It was indeed consecrated three days after Christmas, on the Feast of the Holy Innocents, but the King was not there; he was very ill, and within a few days he died. The first great service held in the new Abbey was his funeral; he was buried before the high Altar. After this there was no peace or happiness in England for many a day. Edward left no son, so the greatest of the English Earls, Earl Harold, was made King. But William, Duke of Normandy, declared that Edward had promised him the crown; and he came across the sea, and fought and killed Harold on the Sussex Hills at the Battle of Hastings. Thus the Norman Duke became William I., King of England, and he was crowned in Westminster Abbey on Christmas Day, 1066. Inside the church with him were the Norman nobles; outside crowded the poor English.

When he was proclaimed King at the Altar, the English shouted, as was their custom, "God save the King!" The Normans within the Abbey heard and wondered. What could the shouts mean? Were the English rising against them? Full of fear and anger they rushed out to find everything in confusion, the houses ablaze, and their men, who had been left outside on guard, killing the poor English. In the Abbey William and the Bishops and monks were left almost alone; and thus, in the gloom and darkness of the winter's day, with the sound of tumult and fighting ringing in their ears, the Conqueror was crowned. This was the first coronation in the Abbey; facing p. 9 is a picture of it.

Two hundred years later King Henry III. pulled down Edward the Confessor's Abbey, and built in its place the Abbey we still have. In it the Confessor's tomb is behind the altar; for Henry had his body reverently moved from its first grave to a chapel which he had especially prepared for it. When you go to the Abbey you will see that this chapel is higher than any of the others; some people say the reason is that, to do more honour to the Confessor, King Henry sent ships to bring earth from the Holy Land, and this sacred earth was piled up into a mound behind the high Altar, and on it the Confessor's chapel was built. This is the part of the Abbey shown in picture 3; turn back and look at it again. Do you see that the old tomb is covered with purple velvet? Are not the pillars and arches about it beautiful?

I have told you only the beginning of the Abbey's history. Not only are all our Kings crowned there but many of them lie buried there too; so also do some of the best and wisest men who have served our country, some of our bravest sailors, and of our greatest poets. Thus it comes about that the history of the Abbey is as long as the history of our country—indeed, it is the history of our country.

III.
THE STORY OF THE CHARTER HOUSE

In 1347 Edward III. was besieging Calais; he was at war with France, and but the year before had won the great victory of Crécy. The siege lasted a whole year, and then at last the men of Calais could hold out no longer, for the French King could not help them and they had no food left. When King Edward heard this he sent to them one of his knights, Sir Walter Manny, with this message, "Give yourselves up to me that I may do with you what I will." This was a hard thing to ask, so hard that Edward's lords pleaded with him to show mercy; and the King gave way and said he would be content if six citizens came to him, barefoot, in their shirts, with ropes about their necks, and bearing the city's keys. "On them," he said, "I will do my will." So the Captain of Calais gave up six of the citizens to Sir Walter Manny, and he brought them to the King and begged him to spare their lives—begged, but begged in vain. Then Queen Philippa, Edward's wife, weeping bitterly, fell on her knees, and prayed the King for love of our Lord to have mercy; and the King's heart was moved to pity, and he answered her, "Though I do it against my will—take them! I give them to you." Can you not fancy how well she treated them, and how happy she was when she sent them home to Calais?

In those days, outside the walls of London towards the north-west was a pleasant land of fields and trees, of streams and clear sweet springs, a lonely land with few houses except three great monasteries. Here Sir Walter Manny and the Bishop of London of that time founded another monastery for twenty-four monks and a Prior or chief monk. It was called the London Charter House, for it was one of several Charter Houses which all belonged to the same kind of monks, who all obeyed the same rules and wore the same dress, and so they are said to belong to the same Order. This new Charter House stood on land which had been given (some by Sir Walter Manny, some by a former Bishop of London,) to be used as a burial-ground for people who had died in the great sickness, called the Black Death, in the year 1349.

NO. 7. OLD PENSIONERS AND SCHOOLBOYS IN THE CHARTER HOUSE. See page <u>28</u>

Let us fancy what the life of the monks of the Charter House was like. Their day began at an hour when you are sound asleep in bed; at eleven o'clock the convent bell rang, and at midnight the monks met in chapel for Matins, their first service, which often lasted two hours, or even longer, so slowly, so solemnly, did they chant the psalms and prayers. When it was over the monks went back to their beds until five o'clock, when they rose and went about the business of the day. What did they find to do? They were busy all day long, for they had to take part in the many services of the chapel; and each monk had his own little house and garden, called his "cell," where he passed most of his time alone. Here he read and prayed; here he worked,—perhaps at carpentering or some such trade, perhaps he copied or wrote books; here he ate his solitary meal, the only meal of the day, which might be of eggs, fish, fruit and vegetables, but never of meat; sometimes it was of bread and water only. By seven o'clock his day was ended and he was asleep in bed. One of the strictest rules of this Order of monks is that they shall be silent except in Chapel. They only meet together twice a week; once when they all dine together, and again on Sundays, when they all go for a long walk in company.

This has been the life of every Carthusian monk (so the Charter House monks are called,) ever since the Order was founded in the eleventh century; and this was the life of the London Charter House from the days of Edward III. until the reign of Henry VIII. Do you remember that he and his Parliament broke the links which bound together the Churches of Rome and England? In 1534 a law was made which said that the King, not the Pope, should henceforth be the Head of the English Church, and that anyone who would not agree to this was a traitor. Some people in England were very glad of this, for there were things in the Church which seemed to them altogether wrong; "Now," they thought, "these wrong things can be set right." But other people were very sorry; they believed the Pope was indeed Head of the whole Church, that God had made him so, and what God had willed man cannot alter. Amongst those who thought so were the monks of the Charter House.

NO. 8. ST. BARTHOLOMEW'S CHURCH BEFORE IT WAS RESTORED. See page <u>30</u>

It is hard to wait day by day for some dreadful thing which we know is surely coming to us, so these were sad days for the monks. Were they frightened, I wonder, when they heard what was going on in the world outside their walls, and knew that soon, very soon, they must tell the fierce King that for them the Pope was and must always be Head of the Church? What would happen to them? Did their prayers and solemn services strengthen and comfort them then? Yes, indeed they did. And their Prior, John Houghton, was a brave true man, as men have need to be in such times; and not only by his words, but by his deeds, he taught his monks to choose rather to die than to give up what they believed to be true; for in the spring of the next year he and two other Carthusian Priors told Thomas Cromwell, the King's great Minister, that they could not change their Faith. They were sent to the Tower, tried as traitors in Westminster Hall, and found guilty. Turn to <u>picture 6</u>; here you see Sir Thomas More, in this month of May himself a prisoner in the Tower for the same reason, watching the three Priors and another monk going away to die. As he watched, More said to his daughter, "Lo, dost thou see, Meg, that these blessed fathers be now as cheerful going to their deaths as bridegrooms to their marriages?"

At Tyburn Tree, where the Marble Arch now stands, John Houghton laid down his life for his Faith.

Two sad years followed; then all but ten of the monks yielded to the King and promised to "forsake the Bishop of Rome." These ten were sent to Newgate Prison. There they would very soon have died, for in those days life in a prison was a dreadful thing, but they were helped by a brave woman, called Margaret Clement, whom Sir Thomas More had brought up with his own daughter Margaret. "Moved with a great compassion of those holy Fathers, she dealt with the gaoler ... and withal did win him with money that he was content to let her come into the prison to them, which she did, attiring and disguising herself as a milkmaid, with a great pail upon her head full of meat, wherewith she fed that blessed company, putting meat into their mouths, they being tied and not able to stir, nor to help themselves."

Soon orders came that the monks were to be kept very strictly, and the gaoler could not allow Margaret Clement to visit them; then, one after another, all but one died.

In 1538 the rest of the monks were turned out of the Charter House. Sorrowfully they passed out under its great archway, and went their different ways to places of safety.

And was the Charter House left empty to fall into ruins? No; it became the property of first one great lord and then of another. They altered it to meet their needs; the monks' cells disappeared; it became a grand mansion. Queen Elizabeth and James I. both stayed there.

At last it was sold to Thomas Sutton, a merchant who had made a large fortune by mining for coal near Newcastle and selling it in London. He must have been a good old man, for we are told he used often to go into his quiet garden to pray, "Lord, Thou hast given me a large and liberal estate; give me also a heart to make use thereof."

He had no children, and when he died, in 1611, he left his great wealth to found a free school, and a "hospital" where eighty old men—"soldiers who had borne arms by land or sea, merchants who had been ruined by shipwreck or piracy, and servants of the King or Queen,"—could spend their last days in peace. They are called the Charter House Pensioners. Turn back to picture 7; these two old men are Pensioners. At first there were to be but forty boys in the school, but the numbers grew larger and larger; and many a great man has been educated in the famous Charter House School.

As the years passed on and London spread beyond its walls, the pleasant fields about the Charter House were covered with streets and houses. At last, about fifty years ago, the Governors of the school thought it would be wise to move it to a more open place; so they built a new school at Godalming in Surrey, and the boys moved into it in 1872. Into the old buildings they had left came a great day-school, the Merchant Taylors', so there are still about 500 boys as well as the old pensioners in the London Charter House.

What a strange history the Charter House has! What changes it has seen! The convent with its silent monks, the great house with its state and royal visitors, the noisy school, the peaceful home of the old pensioners,—the Charter House bears traces of them all. For here are still the courts and cloisters and the chapel of the monks, and the stateroom of the great noble; the boys' playground (picture 2 shows us a little bit of it,) is the square round which once stood the monks' quiet cells; in the chapel we may see the tomb of the Founder, Sir Thomas Sutton; indeed, both the Founders, Sir Thomas Sutton and Sir Walter Manny, lie buried there.

IV.
TWO FAMOUS CHARITIES

Turn to picture 8; this is the ancient church of St. Bartholomew the Great. In it, on the north side of the altar, is an old old tomb on which lies a stone figure in a quaint dress; it is the tomb of Rahere, said to be the founder of the church and of the great Hospital of St. Bartholomew near-by.

This is the story of Rahere:—He was born in France in the reign of William the Conqueror. Early in the twelfth century he was in England, and he was often at the Courts of the Red King and of Henry I. We are told that he was "a pleasant-witted gentleman, and therefore in his time called the Kinge's Minstrell"; indeed, the old chronicler seems to think he led an idle foolish life. If this is true, he certainly repented before long, for he became a pilgrim and made the long and difficult journey to Rome to visit there the places where the Apostles St. Peter and St. Paul were martyred. In Rome he fell ill, and when he was getting better he vowed he would make a hospital "yn re-creacion (that is, re-creation or healing) of poure men."

And now wonderful things happened. In a dream or vision Rahere saw the Apostle Bartholomew, who said to him such words as these:—"Build not only a hospital but also a church, and build them in Smithfield by the City of London." So Rahere went home, called together the citizens of London, and told them what he meant to do. And they answered, "This is a hard thing to compass for Smithfield lieth within the King's market."

Rahere then went to King Henry I. and told him his story, and the King gave him the land he needed,—such land! wet and marshy, "moorish land," an old writer says, "heretofore a common," where the Londoners used to fling out the rubbish and dirt of their city. On this land, in the year 1123, Rahere began to build his hospital, which he called after the Apostle who had appeared to him; and later, as that Apostle had bidden him, he built a Priory; the church you see in picture 8 is part of its church.

Who helped Rahere to do all this? The citizens of London. We are told that he gathered together a crowd of people by pretending to be mad, and then he made them work; they drained the wet marshy soil, they carried great stones, they laboured hard. Thus the hospital was built.

Rahere was its first master. A friend of his, called Alfune, "went himselfe dayly to the Shambles and other markets, where he begged the charity of devout people for their" (that is, the poor sick people's) "reliefe." Now, the charity he asked for was food for them to eat.

Rahere's last years were quietly spent in his own Priory, where he died in the year 1144. This is his story, but it was first written down when writers loved rather to tell wonderful things about great men than to seek out the exact truth about them. Now some people think he did not found the hospital, but both hospital and church are far older than his day; and that the Priory was built for the monks who managed the hospital.

However this may be, the monks of the Priory certainly had great privileges; one of them was that every year, at the Festival of St. Bartholomew, for three days they might hold a fair in the "smooth field" or Smithfield. Have you ever been to a country fair, and seen its funny little stalls of sweets and chinaware and its quaint shows? If you have, you must know that most English fairs are not at all important nowadays; but in the times of which I am writing most of the buying and selling in England was done at them. And so the old writer, Stow, tells us that to St. Bartholomew's Fair "the Clothiers of all England and Drapers of London repayred and had their boothes and standings within the churchyard of this priorie, closed in with walles, and gates locked every night, and watched for safetie of men's goodes and wares"—so rich and valuable was its merchandise. Year by year it was held until 1855; then it was done away with, for serious buying and selling were no longer carried on at such fairs, and "Bartlemy Fair," as it was called, was now famous only for its shows of wild beasts, dwarfs and giants, for its ox roasted whole, and for its scenes of wild merry-making.

For four hundred years the monks of St. Bartholomew's tended the poor people of London. Then came the days when Henry VIII. broke up the monasteries; in 1539 he turned the monks out of the Priory and closed the hospital. Presently I will tell you what afterwards happened to it.

For the beginning of our second charity we must go far away from London to the little town of Assisi in Italy. There, on a spring day of the year 1209, a young man kneeling in a little church heard the priest reading the Gospel for the day:—"As ye go, preach, saying, 'The Kingdom of Heaven is at hand.' Heal the sick, cleanse the lepers.... Provide neither silver nor gold nor brass in your purses, neither scrip nor two coats, nor shoes nor staff." The young man felt as though Christ Himself was speaking to him. "From henceforth," he said, "I shall set myself with all my might to live thus."

NO. 9. AN EXCITING GAME: OLD CHRIST'S HOSPITAL, LONDON

If you had asked the people of Assisi about him, they would have answered you in some such words as these, "Yonder man? He is Francis, the spendthrift son of the cloth-merchant, Pietro Bernardone. He to make such a vow! he, the idle companion of the foolish young nobles of Assisi, the waster of his father's wealth! It is true he has changed of late, but his new way of life pleases his father not at all, for he has given away all he possessed, and says he has taken Poverty as his bride. He visits the lepers, and labours to repair some of the poor churches of the town."

Yet Francis kept his vow. Dressed in a simple grey gown, he went in and out amongst the poorest of the people, preaching to them and tending the sick. In return they could give him but a scanty meal or a night's lodging; money he would not take; it was, he said, of no use to him. And wherever he was, whatever he was doing, no matter what hardships he had to bear—and he had many—he was always full of happiness.

NO. 10. ENTRANCES OF THE OLD CHRIST'S HOSPITAL AND OF CHRIST CHURCH, LONDON

In those hard cruel days men thought little of pain and suffering; but Francis had love and sympathy, not only for men, but for animals and for all things. In one of his poems he calls the moon his sister, and the sun his brother; and he gives thanks for "our sister water, who is very serviceable unto us and humble and precious and clean," and for "our brother fire; he is bright and pleasant and very mighty and strong." We hear of him preaching to the birds, and bidding them be thankful for their feather-clothes and wings.

Soon other men joined themselves to him to live and teach as he did, and they were called Franciscans, the Monks of St. Francis; and sometimes the Grey Friars, because, like St. Francis, they wore grey gowns; and they are also called the Begging Friars, because they too had taken Poverty for their bride, and might own neither houses nor lands; even food they must earn by the labour of their own hands, or kindly people must give it to them. All their time, all their thoughts must be given to helping the poor, the sick, and the wretched; and where they were, there the Friars must go, so they made their homes chiefly in the towns; and at first, while they kept the rules of St. Francis very strictly, even these homes did not really belong to them.

In 1224 nine Franciscans came to England—the very first to come here. Four of them went straight to London. There the poorer people lived on the marshy land near the Thames, huddled together in huts built of mud and wattle; and in such homes there must have been plenty of sickness and misery. For a short time the four Grey Friars lived on Cornhill. Perhaps they thought they had no right to live in so pleasant a place when there was such great misery down by the river; certainly, soon so many people came about them that this first home was too small for them. Now, a London citizen had some property "in Stynkyng Lane and in the parish of St. Nicholas Shambles." Do you know what shambles are? In them animals are killed for food; they cannot be nice places to live in. This property the citizen gave to the Friars, and there they made their new home. By their good deeds they must very quickly have won the respect of the Londoners, for some gave them more lands, and others helped in building a church and monastery for them. This monastery was close to the place where the London General Post Office now stands.

In those days the monasteries did most of the work which is now done by schools, libraries, hospitals, hotels, and workhouses; no doubt the Franciscans did their full share of it in London. But as the years passed on and the first monks died, the younger men who took their places became less strict in keeping the rules of St. Francis; many people gave money and lands to the Order, and it became rich and great, and changed very much. Before a hundred years had passed away, in place of their first church, a new one had been built for them, one of the grandest in the land; its floor and pillars were all of marble. St. Francis told his followers that they needed no books but a Prayer-Book; before long the Grey Friars not only had books, but two hundred years after they settled in London Richard Whittington gave them a library. They no longer gave all their time to caring for the poor and wretched, for we hear of some of them teaching at Oxford and Cambridge; indeed, one of the most learned men of the age, Roger Bacon, was a Grey Friar.

Thus the years passed on until Henry VIII. became King. Do you remember how he treated the monks of the Charter House? I have no such story to tell you of the Grey Friars, for they gave up to the King their monastery and all they possessed when he called on them to do so.

Were the monks missed? Who did the work they had once done? At first much of it was left quite undone. Here is a little bit of a letter which the Lord Mayor of London, Sir Richard Gresham, wrote to the King, in 1538, on this very subject:—Someone, he says, must come to the "ayde and comfort of the poor, syke [sick], blynde, aged and impotent persons beyng not able to help themselffs, nor havyng no place certen where they may be refreshed or lodged at, tyll they be holpen and cured of their diseases and sickness." And he goes on to ask that three ancient hospitals may be given over to the Mayor and Aldermen of the City to carry on once more their old work. King Henry thought this was a wise plan, and in 1546 he gave to London Rahere's old hospital, St. Bartholomew's, and the Grey Friars' monastery.

Nothing more seems to have been done for five years. Yet the poor needed help greatly; and under Henry's son, Edward VI., we hear of sermons being preached, of the King, the Bishop of London, and the Mayor consulting together and making a new plan—that the house of the Grey Friars should be set aside as a hospital or home for "fatherless children and other poore mens children," where they should be fed, clothed, taught, and properly looked after. Thus Edward VI. is often spoken of as the chief founder of the new charity, but I think Henry VIII. and Sir Richard Gresham had more to do with it; don't you? Yet it was the City's charity, and the citizens provided the money needed for it. Before the next winter set in nearly 400 boys and girls were lodged in the old Grey Friars; the next Christmas Day (1552), the children, 340 in number, "all in one livery of russet cotton," lined the road as the Lord Mayor and Aldermen passed in procession to St. Paul's Cathedral. "The next Easter they were in blew [blue] at the Spittle [hospital], and so have continued ever since"; and from these "blew" clothes the school has taken one of its names—the Blue-Coat School. Its other name is Christ's Hospital.

Hundreds of boys have worn the long blue gown and yellow stockings, and some of them have become famous men. I will tell you the name of only one of these, Charles Lamb; for he has written about the school as he knew it, and perhaps you have read Lamb's "Tales from Shakespeare"; he and his sister Mary wrote them.

Facing page 32 is a picture of Blue-Coat boys>, with their gowns tucked up, playing football. Until a short time ago, people in the busy street called Holborn could look through the bars which separated the playground from it, and watch the boys at play. They can do this no longer, for the old buildings have been pulled down, and part of the ground they stood on has been bought for the General Post Office; and in the year 1902 the school, like the Charter House School, moved away into the country, to Horsham.

From the beginning it was meant for girls as well as boys; old papers about it always speak, not of the boys, but of the "children of this House." Boys and girls seem to have lived there, to have dined together in Hall, and even at one time to have shared a classroom for writing-lessons; part of the girls' work was to learn to make their own and the boys' clothes. They too wore a quaint dress with white caps and wide collars, but they gave it up long ago; and long ago, in 1778, they left London; their school is at Hertford. It has never been as famous as the boys' school.

Now I must tell you a little about King Henry's other gift to London, St. Bartholomew's Hospital. It is now one of the largest of the London hospitals, and has become very famous as a school where young men are taught and trained to be doctors; perhaps your doctor was once a student there.

A great part of the Priory church was pulled down as soon as it fell into the hands of Henry VIII., and for many years the rest of it was neglected and allowed to fall almost into ruins. Even in the nineteenth century, stables, coach-houses, and store-rooms stood where once were the monks' old cloisters. In one part of the church was a blacksmith's forge, a fringe factory had taken possession of another, and in still another the boys of the parish school did their lessons. Now all this has been changed. For more than fifty years much care, thought and money have been spent in restoring the building and in getting rid of stables, forge, factory, and school; and now Londoners have every reason to be proud of their beautiful old church.

V.
THE STORY AND HISTORY OF DICK WHITTINGTON

"Turn again, Whittington,
Lord Mayor of London!"

Bow bells sang these words on All-Hallows Day many years ago, and on Highgate Hill a boy stood listening to them. If I ask you who the boy was, I am sure you will answer, "Dick Whittington."

The story of Dick Whittington can be told in two very different ways: there is, first, the old tale which long ago men told their children, and these children told their children. Thus it was passed on from father to son, and we do not know that it was ever written down until the days of James I., nearly two hundred years after Whittington died. Of course, everyone who told this tale wanted to make it as interesting as possible, so little bits were added to it, and it gradually grew more and more wonderful. It is not surprising, then, that learned men have not been satisfied with it, and they have searched the Chronicles and Records of London to find out what they tell us of Richard Whittington, and thus a second story has been made. Now I will tell you first the older story.

Dick Whittington was born in the West of England. While he was still only a little boy his father and mother died, and left him so poor that he had no home, and was thankful to do even the hardest work for just his bare food. One day someone told him that the streets of London were paved with gold. "Can it be true?" he thought to himself. "Is there so much gold in London that it is trodden underfoot? Then it is my own fault if I starve here in the West Country, for am I not big enough and brave enough to tramp all the way up to London? Who could prevent me from picking up some of that gold which surely no one needs, or they would not pave the streets with it? And I need it so much! Courage, Dick Whittington; off with you to London!" So off he set, and tramped all the weary way to the great city.

NO. 11. AN ARCH OF LONDON BRIDGE; TOWER BRIDGE IN THE DISTANCE.

When he reached it, up and down its streets he went,—streets far narrower than those of to-day, and darkened by the overshadowing houses, for often each of their stories stood out a little beyond the story below. Very dirty we should have thought those streets, for people often threw out into them their rubbish and refuse. And what of the gold? Dick saw none. At last, utterly wearied out, utterly disappointed, so weak from hunger that he could hardly stand, he sank down to rest on the doorstep of one of the houses. Now the story says that presently the cook of this house caught sight of him sitting there. She was a bad-tempered woman. She flung open the door and scolded Dick well for an idle fellow, and bade him be off. Dick begged her to give him work so that he might earn some food, but she would not listen to him, and only scolded the more; and while this was going on up came the master of the house, a rich merchant, whose name was Hugh Fitzwarren. He asked the meaning of all these angry words, and he too was vexed to see a boy sitting idly on his doorstep, and bade him go to his work.

"Ah," said Dick, "I have no work, and I have had nothing to eat for three days. I am a poor country lad, and here no one knows me, no one will help me." And he rose up to wander away again, but he was so tired, so weak, he could hardly stand. The merchant saw this, and said to the cook, "Take him in; feed him well, and set him to work to help thee in thy kitchen."

Now, she was, as I said, a bad-tempered woman. Her master's orders she must and did obey, but if Dick now had work and food and a resting-place, he had also many a sharp word, many a sour look, many a cruel blow. Though he worked hard he could not please her. Indeed, in all the household—and it was a large one—the only person who was friendly to him was the merchant's little daughter, Mistress Alice, who not only spoke kindly to him herself, but tried to make his fellow-servants treat him better.

NO. 12. WHITTINGTON SETTING THE KING FREE FROM
THE GREAT DEBT.

Dick slept in a garret which was overrun with rats and mice; they were so
bold that they even crept about over him when he was in bed, and
prevented him sleeping. What could he do about this? In all the world he
had but one penny; how he came by this penny I do not know, but I feel
sure he earned it by doing some extra work. With it he bought a cat and
took her up to his garret, and there she lived and made war on the rats and
mice. Henceforth Dick slept in peace.

Whenever the merchant, Hugh Fitzwarren, sent a ship to trade with foreign
countries, he allowed each of his servants to have some little share in her;
each might send out in her some silk or cloth, or even a very little thing,
whatever he had or could afford to buy; and the money for which this thing
was sold was the servant's own. This the merchant did that "so God might
give him greater blessing." Thus it came about that one day Dick was called
with all the other servants, and each was asked what he would send out in
the good ship Unicorn, which was now ready for sea. When it came to
Dick's turn, he said, "I have nought to send." "Think again," said his
master; "hast thou no little thing thou canst spare? Hast thou nought to
venture?" "Nought, nought," answered Dick, "except my cat, and thou wilt
not take her." "Nay, why not?" said the merchant. "Send thy cat by all
means." So, though his fellow-servants laughed and mocked, Dick's cat was
sent on board the Unicorn.

Now he was lonely indeed; so lonely that the cook's angry words and cross
tempers were harder to bear than ever, and Dick made up his mind to run
away. Very early one morning—it was the Feast of All-Hallows—while his
fellow-servants were still fast asleep, he slipped out of Master Fitzwarren's
house and made his way northward out of London. On Highgate Hill he
sat down to rest. Hark! what was that he heard? Now the wind brought the

sound to him more clearly; now it died away again. It was the chime of Bow bells, and this is what it said to him:—

"Turn again, Whittington,
Lord Mayor of London!"

Lord Mayor of London! Was he to be Lord Mayor? If so, must he not work faithfully, and, if need be, endure hardships—yes, even such little hardships as the cruel words and blows of the bad-tempered cook? Up he jumped, and hurried back so fast that he reached Master Fitzwarren's house before the cook had missed him.

The Unicorn had sailed to the Barbary Coast of Africa. The King of this country was rich and great, yet he was most miserable and uncomfortable, for his kingdom simply swarmed with rats and mice. They were everywhere, even in the beds and on the King's table, where they ate the food which had been prepared for him. When the men of the Unicorn came to the Court to show the King the goods their ship had brought, fancy how surprised they were to see rats and mice here, there, and everywhere! "That cat we have on board," said they, "would soon stop this." "Then let the cat be sent for at once!" cried the King. So Dick's cat was brought, and now in the palace, as once in Dick's garret, she made fierce war on the rats and mice, and before long she had driven them all away. The King was so delighted that he bought the cat for ten times more money than he paid for all the Unicorn's rich merchandise.

When the ship came home, here was fine news for Dick,—no more kitchen-work for him; he was a rich man now. He became a merchant like his master, Hugh Fitzwarren, and by-and-by he married Mistress Alice; and, as Bow bells had promised him, he was made Mayor of London, not once, but three times. He was a good Londoner and a good Englishman, for the story says that when King Henry V. came home after he had conquered France, Whittington entertained him at a great banquet. Look at the picture of this which faces page 41; near the table a fire is burning, and Whittington is just going to throw something into it. How eagerly everyone is watching him, and well they may; for before the King went to France he had borrowed great sums of money from the City and its merchants to pay the cost of his wars, and now Whittington is flinging into the fire the papers in which the King had promised to pay back 37,000 crowns—that is, £60,000 in our money. Thus he set the King free from his debt, or, in other words, gave him all this money. Was not this a princely gift for the great merchant to give the great King?

Now I must tell you what the Chronicles and Records of London tell us about Richard Whittington. He was indeed born in the West of England, but he belonged to a good family. We do not know why and when he came to the City. In those days it was certainly no disgrace for the younger sons of good families to be London merchants; for the City was great and prosperous, able to raise large sums of money to help the King in his wars; and we read that at a council held at the Guildhall about this very matter, to which came the Archbishop of Canterbury and the King's brothers, the Lord Mayor was given the seat of honour above them all, so greatly was he respected because he was London's chief officer.

All the workmen, according to their trades, had to belong to companies called "guilds." Each guild had its own officers and made its own rules for looking after its members; and it had to see not only that these members knew how to do their work, but also that they did it properly and charged a fair price for it. We may still read the rules about all this made by the Guilds of the Blacksmiths, the Plumbers, the Glovers, and many others. Truly, the merchants and workmen of London were honourable and upright, and turned out good honest work. No wonder, then, that Richard Whittington became a London merchant.

He was a mercer—that is, he sold cloth and silk and velvet and such things; and so we hear of him providing velvet for the servants of that Earl of Derby who afterwards became King Henry IV.

Whittington became a great man in the City, was Alderman and Sheriff, and from June, 1397, until November, 1399, he was Mayor. Mayor for a year and five months? Are not Mayors appointed every year in October? and do they not rule only for one year, from November to November? Yes, but the Mayor chosen in October 1396 died during his year of office, and the King, Richard II., appointed Whittington to take his place; and at the year's end the Aldermen chose him to be Mayor again for the next year.

He was still carrying on his business, and when Henry IV. became King, and the Princesses, his daughters, were to be married, Whittington sold to them the cloth of gold and other things necessary for their weddings. He often lent great sums of money to Henry IV., and in later days to his son, Henry V., and in the reign of this King he was Mayor twice. He died in the year 1423; on his gravestone were carved some Latin words which mean that he was the Flower of Merchants. His wife's name was certainly Alice Fitzwarren, but she was the daughter of a Dorsetshire Knight.

So you see the real Richard Whittington was a very great and rich merchant. But many another has been as rich and great, yet no stories are told of them; what makes Whittington different from all others?

First of all, he was Lord Mayor three times, or, rather, may we not say three and a half times? And then he was very wise and generous; he gave, as I have already told you, a library to the Grey Friars; and he arranged that after his death a great deal of his money should be used to help London. His friends, who had to see to this, knew that good water is one of the things most necessary for a great city, so they arched over a spring to keep it clean and sweet, and they placed "drinking-bosses," or taps, in the conduits or channels and pipes which brought the water from country springs and streams into London. Newgate Prison was "feble, over-litel, and so contagious of eyre [air] yat [that] hit caused the deth of many men," so Whittington's money was used to rebuild it. It was also used to repair St. Thomas's Hospital, and to make a new hospital or almshouse where always thirteen old men should live, who were to pray for Dick Whittington's soul, and the souls of his father and mother and wife. These almshouses are no longer in the City; they have been moved out to Highgate, and stand not far from the stone which marks the place where Whittington heard the chime of Bow bells; and through them Dick Whittington's wealth is still doing good to the poor of London.

VI.
WHEN ELIZABETH WAS QUEEN

In the reign of Henry VI., Humphrey, Duke of Gloucester, the King's uncle, built himself a palace at Greenwich, and he called it "Placentia" or "Plaisance," which means a pleasant thing or place. (Turn over this page and the next, and you will find a picture of it.) I think the Tudor Kings really found it a pleasant place, for they lived there a great deal; here Henry VIII. and his daughters, Mary and Elizabeth, were born, and here Edward VI. died.

In those days the road we now call the Strand led from the City to the village of Charing Cross; and all along it stood great and beautiful houses with gardens which stretched down to the river. Each house, most likely, had its water-gate or landing-place, where the master of the house and his guests could step on board their barges, which might take them up the river to Westminster and the royal palace near Richmond, or down to London and beyond it to Greenwich; for in those days the river was London's greatest and most stately highway. Very stately were the barges, very gay, too, with flags and the fine liveries of servants; and very often people on the banks or in little boats near-by heard music sounding from their decks as they moved swiftly along. How beautiful, how stately, must Queen Elizabeth's barge have been, when at her Coronation she came by water to the Abbey!

She often stayed in her palace called Plaisance; how grandly she lived there! One who saw her there tells of the "gentlemen, barons, earls, Knights of the Garter, all richly-dressed and bareheaded," who went before her; one of them carried the sceptre, another the sword of state. The ladies of her Court followed her, and she was guarded on each side by fifty gentlemen who carried gilt battle-axes. She was herself magnificently dressed, and "wherever she turned her face as she passed along, everybody fell down on their knees."

NO. 13. GREENWICH AS IT IS NOW.

Sometimes, when she wanted to be amused, plays were acted in the great hall of the palace, and she sat in her chair of state with her ladies about her and looked on. I wonder if any of these plays were written by Shakespeare? Perhaps they were; it is even possible that Shakespeare himself may have acted before her, for he had come to London from his country home two years before the Spanish Armada sailed up the English Channel to conquer England; and during the last five years of her reign, whenever Elizabeth went up the river in her barge, she passed the round wooden theatre, called the Globe, where his plays were acted, for it was in Southwark on the south bank. There is no sign of it now; a great brewery has been built over the place where once it stood.

These were the days when English sailors fought the Spanish on the high seas, because they claimed all the New World as their own and strove to keep everyone else out of it. From the windows or the terrace of her palace did the Queen ever watch ships sailing down the river to take part in this struggle, or in another,—a struggle with winds and waves, ice and snow, as the sailors tried to explore the unknown coasts of America? Once at least we know she did, for Admiral Frobisher's two little ships fired a salute to her as they dropped down the river. He was going to search for gold and for the North-West Passage round the north of America to the Pacific. He found no passage and no gold though he went again and yet again to the cold North. How often Englishmen searched for that passage; how hard they found it to believe that there is no way for ships through those icy seas!

PL. 14. PLACENTIA, THE OLD PALACE OF GREENWICH

NO. 14. PLACENTIA, THE OLD PALACE AT GREENWICH.

Those were stirring times. Often sailors came home with wonderful tales to tell; and thus, in September, 1580, a ship, called the Pelican, sailed into Plymouth Sound, and all England rang with the news of her coming, for she was Admiral Drake's ship. Nearly three years before he and his sailors had left England in her; they had fought the Spanish, they had taken great treasure, money and jewels, and they had sailed round the world. Now they were safe home again. Do you wonder that the Queen wanted to see the ship which had made such a voyage? She told Drake to bring the Pelican round to Deptford, which is very near Greenwich; and she went on board and took part in a great feast which was given in her honour; and she knighted Drake on the deck of his own ship. How proud Englishmen were of him! One of them said the Pelican ought to be hoisted up to the top of the tower of St. Paul's Cathedral, to take the place of the spire which had been destroyed by lightning some time before. Was not this a mad plan? Of course, it was never carried out. For many a year the old ship lay in Deptford Dockyard just as the Victory lies now in Portsmouth Harbour; and people used to visit her, and even have supper on board her. When she was very old she was broken up; out of some of her timbers a chair was made and presented to Oxford University.

Do you remember what happened in 1588? This was the year of the Invincible Armada, when England had to prepare ships and sailors and soldiers to protect herself from the Spanish. What help did London give? She was asked for fifteen ships and five thousand men. "Give us two days," said her citizens, "to consider what we can do"; and in two days they answered, "We will send thirty ships and ten thousand men to serve our country."

London, then, had certainly plenty of ships; and many a sea-captain besides Frobisher sailed down the river past Placentia on his way to some far-off port; for London merchants were eager to trade with all parts of the world; and after the defeat of the Spanish Armada they knew that the wide ocean, east and west, lay open before them. No Spaniard now could forbid English ships to sail on any sea.

Drake had seen for himself and had brought home word of the spices and great wealth of the East Indies. But they were very far off, and the cost of fitting out ships for so long a voyage was very great; great, too, were the dangers these ships would have to face—dangers of sea and storm, of savage people and an unknown land; could any one merchant risk so much? The Lord Mayor called together some London merchants to consider this question, and they answered, "The losses which would ruin one would hardly be felt if borne by many; let us, then, form a company to trade with the East." Thus began the East India Company; its birthday was the very last day of the sixteenth century. It had at first only four ships and less than five hundred men; before it came to an end, two hundred and fifty-eight years later, it was ruling nearly all India.

I have another story to tell you which began nearly twenty years before the East India Company's birthday. In December, 1581, a young man came to Placentia, bringing letters to the Queen from her soldiers in Ireland, where there had been war and great trouble. He was carefully dressed and wore a new plush cloak, for this was, I think, his first visit to Court, and the Queen loved to see everyone about her well and beautifully dressed. Perhaps he had only just arrived; perhaps the Queen had been out in her barge and was coming up from the riverside to her palace; however it may have been, she came to a very muddy place in the road, which is not at all surprising, since in December there is often a great deal of rain. The Queen looked at the puddles and stopped, and the young man sprang forward, swept his plush cloak from his shoulders and spread it over the mud for her to step on that so she might pass on without soiling her shoes. I feel sure you know the young man's name—it was Walter Raleigh. Is it any wonder that he became a great favourite with the Queen? An old story says that soon after this he wrote with a diamond on the glass of a window in the palace:—

"Fain would I climb, yet fear to fall."

And the Queen saw it, and wrote beneath it:—

"If thy heart fail thee, climb not at all."

His heart did not fail him; he became captain of her Guard, and he rose higher and higher in her service.

Raleigh was the first Englishman to think how splendid it would be if some of his countrymen would go to America and make homes for themselves there, and so build up a greater England beyond the seas. He sent out ships to explore, and twice he sent out men to settle in the new land. Some the Indians killed; some found the work of building houses and clearing away the forests far harder than they had expected; and the Indians often attacked them, and food was sometimes so scarce they almost died of hunger. Do you wonder they lost heart and came back to England? Thus it seemed that Raleigh's plan quite failed; but it did not really, for about twenty years later, a company, like the East India Company, was formed, called the Virginia Company. It sent out some settlers who sailed from London in the year 1606, and they did what Raleigh's men had failed to do—built themselves homes, and cleared and tilled the land. Thus began the British Dominions beyond the Seas.

One thing Raleigh did which must not be forgotten. The men he sent to explore in America saw potatoes and tobacco growing there, and learnt from the Indians how to use them. When they came home they showed Raleigh the plants they had brought back with them. He tried smoking tobacco, and I think he must have liked it very much, for he used to give his friends pipes with silver bowls and teach them how to smoke. And he planted potatoes in the garden of a house he had in Ireland; his were the very first Irish potatoes. A few years later both potatoes and tobacco were growing in the garden of one of those fine houses in the Strand of which I have told you; people thought them very rare and curious plants.

Eight years before the great Queen died, Raleigh went himself to South America, and sailed far up the River Orinoco. He found a fertile land and friendly Indians, who told him wonderful stories of the great "city of Manoa" which was (so they said,) rich beyond the dreams of man; El Dorado, the Golden City, the Spanish called it. Raleigh never forgot these stories; more than twenty years later they helped to bring him back to America.

When Elizabeth died and James I. came to the throne he fell into disgrace, for some people said he had plotted against the King; so he was tried, found guilty, and condemned to death. But he was not killed; year after year he was kept a prisoner in the Tower of London. How did he pass his days there? was he very dull and sad? I think not. Part of the time his wife and son lived with him; he was very much interested in the new science of chemistry, and he worked at it and tried experiments in his cell; he began to write a wonderful History of the World; and I think he thought and dreamed much about Manoa, his Golden City, and the riches which lay hidden in South America. The Spanish said these riches were all theirs; but Raleigh did not believe this, and he thought Englishmen could so easily get possession of some of them. After many years he tried to persuade King James to let him cross the Atlantic and sail up the Orinoco to find a gold-mine he had heard of there; he said if only he might go and open it up, it would bring great wealth to the King. Had he another hope, I wonder, hidden away in his heart, of which he did not speak—that he might also search for and find his Golden City? However this may be, he certainly tried to persuade the King, and he succeeded, for James said, "Yes, you may go," though he well knew that Raleigh could not go to South America and bring home gold without offending the Spanish, and England was then at peace with Spain. So Raleigh sailed away. After fifteen months he came home with a sad tale to tell;—everything had gone wrong, the Spanish had killed many of his men, and he had found no gold. James sent him back to the Tower; and four months later, in the year 1618, he was beheaded, because (so he was told,) he had once plotted against the King. Thus died the last of the great men of Queen Elizabeth's Court who had done so much for England.

How different London is now from the London of Queen Elizabeth's reign! Old St. Paul's and its high tower,—I will tell you in the next story what became of them. The Globe Theatre, too, has quite disappeared. Busy shops have taken the places of the beautiful old houses in the Strand; nothing now reminds us of them except the names of some of the streets which turn off it; and Somerset House, the great building where now some of the business of the nation is carried on, is so called because it stands on the place where the Duke of Somerset, who lived in Edward VI.'s reign, began to build a palace for himself. If you go down the river to Greenwich, will you see Queen Elizabeth's pleasant palace? Ah, no. Sixty years after she died it was so out of repair that Charles II. ordered it to be pulled down and a new one built in its place. This new palace was not finished until William and Mary's reign. Then there was a great war with France, and the Queen begged the King to finish the palace and to turn it into a hospital for sailors who had been wounded or crippled in one of the great sea-fights. So it came to pass that, instead of Placentia, we now have Greenwich Palace; you will find a picture of it facing p. 48.

Perhaps you are thinking, "At any rate the Tower has not changed, and London still has a Lord Mayor." But even the Tower has changed, for in Queen Elizabeth's time it was a royal palace as well as a prison. She did not use it often; perhaps she did not like it, for she had been a prisoner there herself when her sister Mary was Queen. Now our Kings never live there; and prisoners are not kept there; and for more than a hundred and fifty years no one has been beheaded there. I must tell you of one other change, for I am sure it will interest all children. In Queen Elizabeth's reign, if you had gone to see the Tower, you would have been shown also the lions and other wild animals which, from very early times, had been kept there in dens near the part which is called, after them, the Lion Tower. Now you must go to the Zoological Gardens to see wild animals; there are none in the Tower; they were all sent away to the Zoo not long before Queen Victoria began to reign.

NO. 15. THE FIRE OF LONDON

From the Fresco by Stanhope A. Forbes, R.A., in the Royal Exchange

By permission of the Artist and the Sun Insurance Office

See page 61

As for the Lord Mayor, he is still the first magistrate of London, and he still takes the leading place in all London's affairs, just as he did in Queen Elizabeth's reign. No, his work and duties have not changed, except that, as London has grown greater and more important, they have grown greater and more important also.

VII.
ST. PAUL'S CATHEDRAL

The Cathedral of the City of London is called St. Paul's. In the picture beside this page you can see its great dome and golden cross, the top of which is nearly as many feet above the ground as there are days in the year. For more than thirteen hundred years God has been worshipped on the spot where St. Paul's now stands; before that, many people think, a Roman temple stood there; and before that, again, perhaps the ancient Londoners worshipped there the God Lud, of whom I have told you; since that time the number of the years has grown from hundreds to thousands.

NO. 16. ST. PAUL'S FROM THE RIVER

Let us fancy what this country was like more than thirteen hundred years ago. The English had conquered it and given it their name and language. The Christian Faith, which the Britons had learnt while the Romans were ruling them, had been almost quite forgotten except in the western part of the land; for in the east very many of the English had settled, and they were heathen. Do you remember that Pope Gregory the Great, when he was still just a simple priest, had seen some English children in the slave-market at Rome, and thought they were fair as angels? He never forgot these children, and when he became Pope he sent his friend, Augustine, and some priests to England to teach its people the Christian Faith. These missionaries landed in Kent and were kindly received by its King, Ethelbert, whose wife, Bertha, was already a Christian. In time he was baptized; and the old historian Bede tells us that he "builded in the Citie of London St. Paules Church"; and its first Bishop was that Mellitus to whom the fisherman Edric brought the message that St. Peter had consecrated his own abbey on Thorney.

In time Ethelbert died, and Mellitus was made Archbishop of Canterbury; then the men of London became heathen again. There is a curious old tale about this, and though it is just a story, not real history, I will tell it to you. Do you remember that the monks said Sebert, King of the East Saxons, rebuilt St. Peter's Abbey? Do you not think, then, that he must have cared enough about the Christian Faith to teach it to his sons? Yet after his death they went back to the old Faith. It chanced that one day, when Mellitus was holding the solemn service of the Mass, they broke open the door of the church, rushed in and ordered him to give them "white bread" such as he used to give their father; they meant the Bread used in the Mass. How could Mellitus give it to men who did not believe the Faith in which such Bread is a holy thing? He refused, and in their anger they turned him out of London; and, as I said, the Londoners went back to their old religion. Truly it took a long time and much teaching to make them really Christians.

Near the end of the seventh century we hear of another Bishop of London, called Erkenwald. He did much to make St. Paul's beautiful and splendid. And he cared for his people too,—the men, women and children, who lived scattered about in the wild forests which then lay round London; and in order that he might visit, help and teach them, he used to drive in a cart from place to place over rough roads, and often where there were no roads. He was so good that people said he was a saint; and so when he died and his body was buried in St. Paul's, his grave there was greatly honoured,—it was even said that miracles were worked there. Is it there still? Ah, no; it was destroyed long ago, as you shall hear presently. Yet London ought not to forget this old Bishop since it is said that one of her streets is called after him, for in his days it seems that the old Roman walls had fallen into ruins, and it is said that Erkenwald built a new city-gate ever since called, after him, Bishopsgate. If you look at a map which shows the streets of London, you will find Bishopsgate and Bishopsgate Street near Liverpool Street Station. This story shows us that Erkenwald was a good citizen as well as a good Bishop.

The years passed on; the Normans came and conquered England; and now we have come to real history.

Near the end of William I.'s reign, St. Paul's was burnt down, and the Bishop of London of that day began to build in its place a cathedral so grand and large that men thought it would never be finished, "it was to them so wonderful for height, length, and breadth." Yet little by little it grew until—but not for more than two hundred and twenty-five years—it stood complete with its great steeple, the highest in Europe, towering up 520 feet into the air. This is the Cathedral to which in later days Queen Elizabeth came to return thanks to God for the defeat of the Spanish Armada. Here Sir Philip Sidney was buried. Perhaps you remember that, as he lay dying on a battlefield in the Netherlands, someone brought him a drink of cold water which seemed to him the most delicious thing in all the world, so thirsty was he because of his wounds. Then he saw a poor soldier looking at it with longing eyes, and he would not drink it, "for," he said, "his need is greater than mine; give it to him."

In the days of Oliver Cromwell the poor Cathedral was used as a barrack for soldiers and as a stable for their horses. There is now in the British Museum a printed paper ordering the soldiers not to play nine-pins and other games there between nine o'clock at night and six in the morning, because their noise and shouts while they played greatly disturbed the people who lived near the churchyard. Long before this the great steeple had been struck by lightning and burnt down, and the whole Cathedral had fallen out of repair; thus, when Cromwell died and Charles II. became King, there was much talk as to what was to be done for it.

OLD ST. PAUL'S.
Burnt down in 1666.

OLD ST. PAUL'S. Burnt down in 1666.

The summer of the year 1666—the year after the Great Plague—was very hot; an east wind blew for weeks together, so the old crowded wooden houses of the City must have been as dry as tinder, when, on September 2, a fire broke out in a baker's shop in Pudding Lane. At first, I suppose, the neighbours watched it and thought it just such a fire as they had seen many a time before; but how could they have felt when it spread from house to house, and leapt from street to street? when days passed and still it spread? Some people ran about like distracted creatures, not even trying to save their possessions; others fled away to the fields outside the City, carrying with them all they could. Imagine them huddling under the hedges for shelter and looking back at the crimson sky, for an old writer tell us "all the sky was of a fiery aspect like the top of a burning oven, and the light" was "seen above forty miles round about for many nights." The melting lead of the roof of St. Paul's ran "down the streets in a stream, and the very pavements were glowing with a fiery redness, so as no horse or man was able to tread on them." Five days the fire raged. When at last it died out, London lay in ruins; 400 streets, 89 churches and 4 of the city-gates had been burnt, besides the Cathedral, and in it the shrine of St. Erkenwald.

Has any city, I wonder, ever suffered so great a loss? Were the Londoners sad and miserable when they looked at the ruins? For a time, perhaps, they were; but soon they set themselves to build a new London with wider streets and houses made of stone, which would not burn so easily; and the man who advised and helped them most to do this was Sir Christopher Wren. He drew the plans for, and saw to the rebuilding of, many of the city churches, and above all of the Cathedral. Look again at its picture facing page 57. The first of its stones was laid in June, 1675, and the last and highest in 1710; but it is not finished even yet; month by month the work goes on. If you go into it, you will see men busy covering its great walls and pillars with beautiful rich colours.

Wren lived to be a very old man. Towards the end of his life he used to come to London once a year to sit for awhile under the great dome which he had planned and built, for he loved it, and I think it was to him not only a beautiful, but also a solemn and a holy thing. When he died his body was buried in the Cathedral; his name and what he did are written over the north door, and also some Latin words which mean, "Reader, if thou seekest his monument, look around."

St. Paul's has taken part in our life as a nation ever since. Here some of our greatest men are buried. Nelson and Wellington both lie here, and so do some other great British sailors and soldiers, some also of our statesmen and painters; and monuments have been put up here in memory of others whose graves are far away. Here Queen Victoria came in 1897 to return thanks to God for her long reign; and here every day, and especially on Sundays and on all great national occasions, solemn services of prayer and supplication, or of praise and thanksgiving, are held.

Milton Keynes UK
Ingram Content Group UK Ltd.
UKHW040839141024
449705UK00006B/388